Around the World
Schools

Margaret Hall

Heinemann
LIBRARY

www.heinemann.co.uk/library
Visit our website to find out more information about **Heinemann Library** books.

To order:
☎ Phone +44 (0)1865 888066
📄 Send a fax to +44 (0)1865 314091
💻 Visit the Heinemann Bookshop at www.heinemann.co.uk/library to browse our catalogue and order online.

First published in Great Britain by Heinemann Library, Halley Court, Jordan Hill, Oxford
OX2 8EJ, a division of Reed Educational and Professional Publishing Ltd. Heinemann
is a registered trademark of Reed Educational and Professional Publishing Ltd.

OXFORD MELBOURNE AUCKLAND JOHANNESBURG BLANTYRE
GABORONE IBADAN PORTSMOUTH NH (USA) CHICAGO

Designed by Lisa Buckley
Originated by Dot Gradations
Printed in Hong Kong/China

ISBN 0431 15132 6 (hardback)   ISBN 0431 15137 7 (paperback)
06 05 04 03 02   07 06 05 04 03 02
10 9 8 7 6 5 4 3 2   10 9 8 7 6 5 4 3 2 1

British Library Cataloguing in Publication Data

Hall, Margaret
 Schools. – (Around the world)
 1. Schools – Juvenile Literature
 I. Title
 394.2'6

Acknowledgements

The publishers would like to thank the following for permission to reproduce photographs: Title page, p.10 Sovfoto/Eastfoto/
PictureQuest; p.4 © Wolfgang Kaehler; p.5 Michael Dwyer-Stock, Boston, Inc./PictureQuest; p.6 John Elk/Stock, Boston; p.7 © Nik
Wheeler; p.8 Helga Lade/Peter Arnold, Inc.; p.9 Jacques Jangoux-Stock Connection/PictureQuest; p.11 Bill Bachmann/The Image
Works; p.12 Mark Edwards-Still Pictures/Peter Arnold, Inc.; p.13 Jeff Greenberg/Peter Arnold, Inc.; p.14 Shehzad Noorani-Still
Pictures/Peter Arnold, Inc.; p.15, Bob Daemmrich/Stock, Boston, Inc.; p.16 David Klammer/The Image Works; p.17 Lionel
Coates/Bruce Coleman Inc.; p.18 Elizabeth Crews/The Image Works; p.19 Michael Wolf-Visum/The Image Works; p.20 Dean
Conger/Corbis; p.21 Paul A. Souders/Corbis; p.22 South American Pictures; p.23 J. Schytte-Still Pictures/Peter Arnold, Inc.; p.24 James
Marshall/The Image Works; p.25 Bob Daemmrich/The Image Works; p.26 © Victor Englebert; p.27 Ken Heyman/Woodfin Camp and
Associates; p.28 Don L. Boroughs/The Image Works; p.29 Howard Davies/Corbis.

Cover photograph reproduced with permission of Earl and Nazima Kowell/Corbis.

Every effort has been made to contact copyright holders of any material reproduced in this book. Any omissions will be rectified in
subsequent printings if notice is given to the publishers.

Contents

Some words are shown in bold, **like this.** You can find out what they mean by looking in the glossary.

Schools around the world

All around the world, children go to
school. Some children spend most of their
day at school. Others spend only a few
hours there.

Schools are different in different parts of the world, but they are all the same in one way. Schools are where children go to learn.

School buildings

The kind of school buildings children go to depends on where they live. It depends on the **climate** and the **resources** of their community.

School buildings can be large or small. They can be made from many different materials. Some children even go to school outside, or in buildings with no walls.

Getting to school

Children travel to school in many different ways. The kind of **transport** they use depends on where they live. It also depends on how far they have to go.

Many children walk or ride bicycles to school. Others ride in cars, on buses, or on trains. Some children go to school by boat.

School clothing

Children around the world wear different kinds of clothing to school. What they wear often depends on the **climate** where they live. It also depends on what **season** it is.

In some schools, the children all dress alike. They wear **uniforms**. Students from different schools have different uniforms.

The school day

All around the world, teachers help **pupils** learn new things. Children do some schoolwork in groups. They do other schoolwork on their own.

Most children eat lunch or a snack at school. They may also have time to play. Many children go on school trips, too.

Learning to read and write

One important job for teachers is to help children learn to read and write. Around the world, different **languages** are written using different letters.

The language children use at school depends on where they live. Some children learn their own language and learn another language as well.

Other lessons

Children learn many things at school.
All around the world, they study maths
and science. They learn about their
own country and other countries, too.

Many children around the world study art and music in school. They may also learn how to work on a computer.

School jobs

Most children have jobs to do at school.
They help to keep the classroom neat
and clean. They may even help to set up
the classroom every day.

In some places, children work to keep the playground neat and clean. Some children may serve lunch to one another.

After school

Some children have more lessons after the school day is over. They may have a **tutor** to help them with the subjects that they find hard. They may have homework to do.

Some children learn different things after school. They may learn about dance, music or their own **culture**.

Special schools

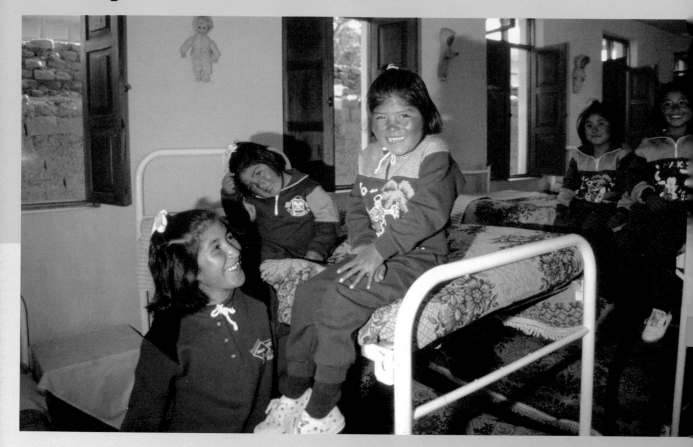

Some children live at their school. Schools like this are called **boarding schools**. The children only go home for visits and on holidays.

This boy is **blind**. He goes to a school where he can learn in special ways. Some people who are blind read with their fingers. They use an **alphabet** of raised dots which they can feel. It is called **Braille**.

Home schooling

A home can also be a school. Children may live too far from a school to go there every day. Some parents teach their children at home because they want to decide exactly what their children learn.

People at schools will often help parents plan home lessons for their children. Many children who study at home go to a school for gym or art classes.

School and work

In some places, children must help their families earn money. They go to school for only part of the day. Then they work for part of the day.

Some children work as **performers**. They spend part of their day **practising** the skills they perform. They spend the rest of the day studying ordinary school subjects.

Older students

Many people go to school even when they are **adults**. They may go to **college**. They may go on a course to learn how to do a certain job.

Adults also take classes for fun. They study different **languages** and learn how to do things. No matter how old **students** are, they go to school to learn.

Photo list

Glossary

adult grown-up

alphabet letters or signs of a language

blind cannot see

boarding school school where children also live

Braille an alphabet of raised dots used by people who cannot see

climate normal type of weather for an area

college place where older students learn

culture things that a group of people does and believes in

language system of words people use to speak, write and read

performer someone who does something like dancing or acting, for others to watch

practise do something over and over to get better at it

resource something available for people to use

season time of the year, like winter, spring, summer or autumn

student someone who has finished school and carries on learning at a college or university

transport ways to move people and things from place to place

tutor teacher who works with a pupil or small group outside the classroom

uniform clothing that is all the same to show that a person is a member of a certain school or group

More books to read

Emily's first 1000 days at school by Rosemary Wells, Hyperion, 2000

Going on a school trip by D. Church, Franklin Watts, 2000

School by Jane Shuter, Heinemann Library, 1998

School by Kath Cox and Pat Hughes, Hodder Wayland, 1997

School days by B.G. Hennessy, Picture Puffins, 1992

Index